FUN & EASY
Origami
Animals

Full-Color Instructions for Beginners

Michael G. LaFosse

TUTTLE Publishing

Tokyo │ Rutland, Vermont │ Singapore

contents

PENGUIN
12

FLAPPING BIRD
8

SKUNK
10

OWL
18

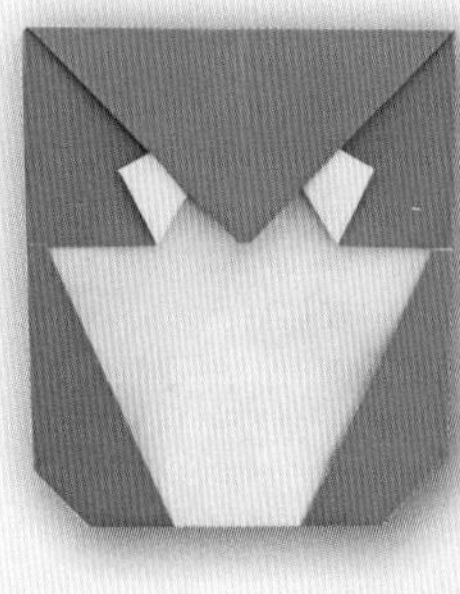

WHALE
14

BAT
16

JAGUAR
20

SWAN
22

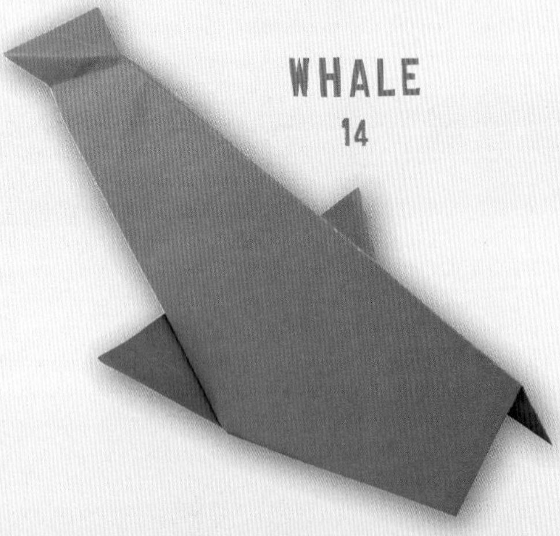

CRANE
24

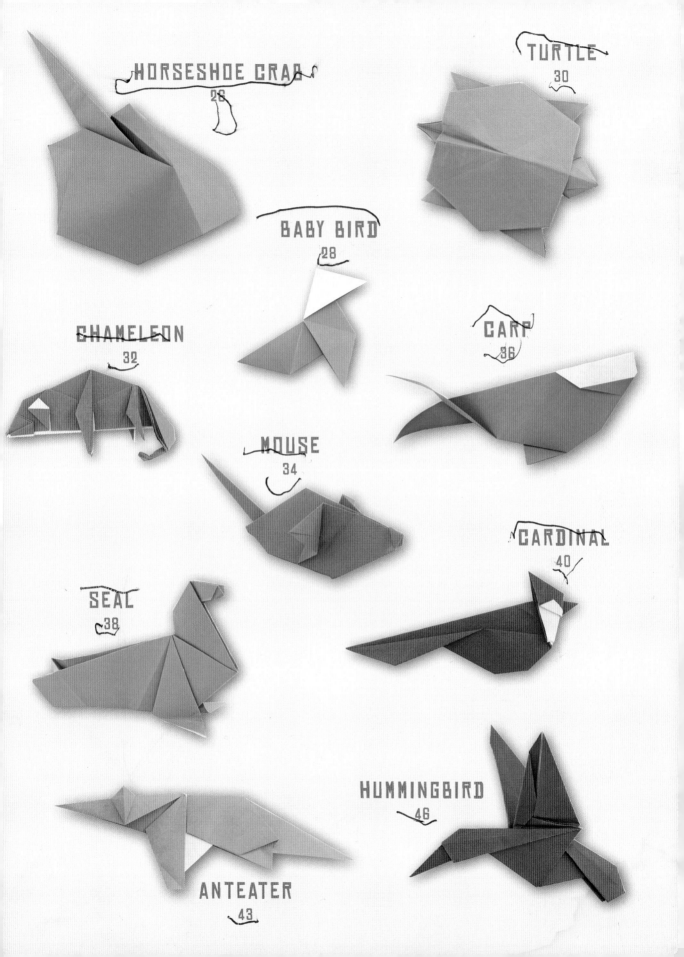

HORSESHOE CRAB
28

TURTLE
30

BABY BIRD
28

CHAMELEON
32

CARP
36

MOUSE
34

CARDINAL
40

SEAL
38

HUMMINGBIRD
46

ANTEATER
43

INTRODUCTION

The idea of folding paper is as old as paper itself. Think of the advantages to early folders: Folding a message kept its contents secret. Wrapped goods stayed clean and fresh. Written accounts were more convenient to carry and read when folded into a book, instead of being rolled into a scroll.

With the development of origami, paper became much more than a simple wrapper or convenience. The artful folds form models that garner admiration and inspire imitation. Beautiful patterns emerge, and representations of living things and familiar or clever objects take form.

Origami is wonderfully simple. The folder needs nothing more than something to fold—no glue or tape—just paper! Origami exemplifies the mind's ability to solve problems and create harmony. Folding is relaxing, but it is also exciting to invent new ways to fold paper.

The Chinese are credited with the invention of paper, and they were probably the first to create folded paper designs. But today, paper folding is known the world over by its Japanese name. This is thanks to the venerable Japanese origami crane, one of the most popular designs ever made. When modern folders needed a simple word for their art, they looked to Japan, the home of the folded paper crane, and came up with *origami*. In Japanese *ori* means "to fold" and *kami* means "paper."

ORIGAMI PAPER

Choosing the best paper for a particular project can be as important as the folding process itself. Here are some things to consider:

Paper for learning and practicing origami does not have to be fancy or expensive. Look for papers that are fairly thin, like copier paper or sheets cut from the pages of discarded magazines. You must, of course, prepare your papers: cut them carefully to make perfect squares.

When you're ready to build a collection of fine folding papers, you'll discover many options that you can order online: machine made and handmade, in rolls or sheets, and in many colors, patterns, and sizes.

Terazaki / Wikimedia Commons (by way of The Metropolitan Museum of Art, a gift of Lincoln Kirstein, 1959) / Public Domain

HOW TO FOLD 1

Recognizing the Symbols

By making this simple Flower Bud you will learn how to recognize the origami diagram symbols listed at right.

- Valley fold
- Mountain fold
- Follow this spot
- Rotate symbol
- Fold and unfold arrow
- Fold in front arrow
- Fold behind arrow

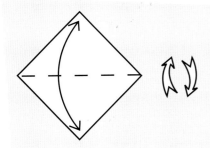

1 Begin with a square piece of paper, plain side up if you are using origami paper. Fold the paper in half bottom corner to the top corner, and then unfold. Here you see what the valley fold (dashed line) is and what the fold and unfold arrow looks like. Next, notice the rotate symbol to the right of the diagram. This indicates that you must position your paper to look like step 2 (with the crease running vertically) before making the next fold.

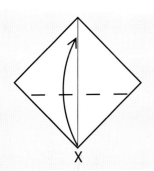

2 By now, you should have rotated your paper so that the crease made in step 1 is running from the top corner to the bottom corner. Now lift up the bottom corner to make a fold, but do not lift it all the way to the top. See the X, "follow this spot," at the bottom corner. You need to look ahead to step 3 to see where the X should go.

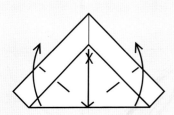

3 Fold up the left and right sides. Here, there is no X on the left and right sides. Even without the X, it is a good habit to look ahead to the next step, so you will be able to see what the paper should look like.

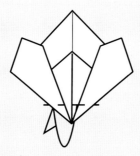

4 Fold the bottom corner to the back. Here, you see the mountain fold indicator (a broken dashed line) and the open half arrow indicating that you should "fold behind."

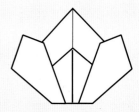

5 Now you have the finished Flower Bud! Make several tiny buds from two-inch square papers and paste them onto the front of a handmade card, or save them to decorate another project.

HOW TO FOLD 2

Practicing Neat Folding

Neatness is important when you are folding. This simple exercise will help you practice matching edges—a straightforward task but a common problem for many beginners who do not realize how important it will become later on.

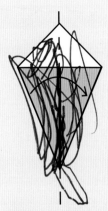

3 Fold the Kite Base in half, left to right. This is a good way to check for neatness. Do all of the edges match? Are the corners neat?

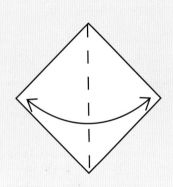

1 Begin with a square of paper, plain side up if you are using origami paper. Fold it in half corner to corner, and then unfold. Be sure to match the corners and the edges of the square carefully before you press the paper flat to "commit" the crease.

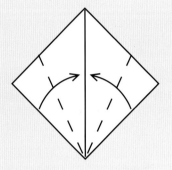

2 Fold the two bottom edges to meet at the crease in the center. For neatness, fold only one side at a time. Leave an approximately one-millimeter gap between the two folded flap edges (to facilitate the fold in step 3), but be sure that the edges of the paper align with the crease exactly before you press the paper flat. This shape is often called the "Kite Base." Many origami designs begin from this basic shape.

4 Make several of these and use them to practice inside-reverse folding, as explained in the next section, where you will make an origami Duck!

How did you do? If your shape is not very good, try to figure out what went wrong. Perhaps your paper is the problem. Check to see if it is really square. If the paper is square, perhaps your first fold, from step 1, was done poorly—every fold counts! Try again. Practice will help you improve your basic folding skills. Teaching others what you have learned will improve these skills, too.

HOW TO FOLD 3
Learning the Inside-Reverse Fold

In this section you will practice the inside-reverse fold. This is an important origami technique that, with a little practice, will allow you to complete many origami designs. The inside-reverse fold is most often used to make bends in the paper for the joints of the limbs, neck, and head of an origami animal.

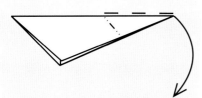

1 Begin with a Kite Base folded in half (see the previous section for the folding method). Here you see a typical drawing of an inside-reverse fold instruction. Look at step 4 to see what the paper should look like once it has been inside-reverse folded. Notice that the corner has been bent inside itself.

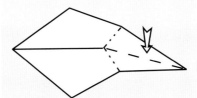

2 Begin the fold by opening the Kite Base from underneath. Now you can easily push the narrow end downward. Notice that only part of the Kite Base will be valley folded, from the bend in the middle to the end of the point.

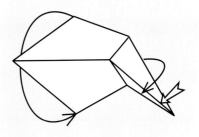

3 Once the valley fold portion of the fold is started, you can begin to fold the shape flat (in half) again. You can push the bent point to any angle you want.

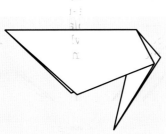

4 This is what a completed inside-reverse fold should look like.

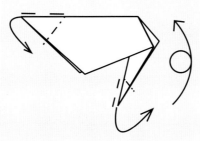

5 Try adding two more inside-reverse folds, one at the left end and another at the end of the first point. Notice the turn-paper-over symbol, which tells you that after you make the inside-reverse folds, you should turn the paper over so it looks similar to the next drawing.

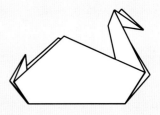

6 This is your finished Duck! Make many of them to become an expert at inside-reverse folding.

FLAPPING BIRD

Traditional Japanese design

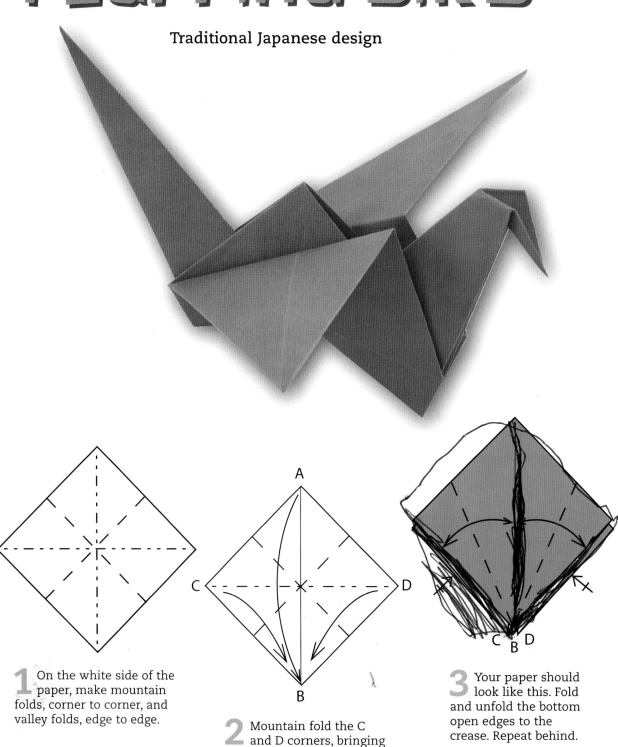

1 On the white side of the paper, make mountain folds, corner to corner, and valley folds, edge to edge.

2 Mountain fold the C and D corners, bringing A, C, and D down to B.

3 Your paper should look like this. Fold and unfold the bottom open edges to the crease. Repeat behind.

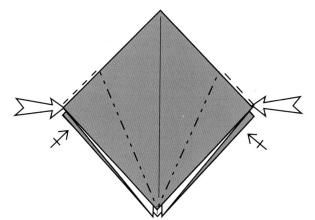

4 Push in the corners, following the creases from step three. Repeat behind.

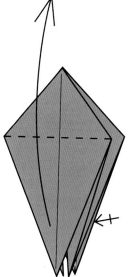

5 The front and back flaps should now be free. Fold up the front flap. Repeat behind.

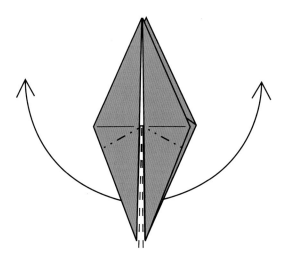

6 Inside-reverse fold the bottom corners, one to the right and one to the left.

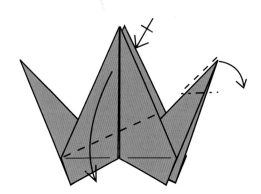

7 Inside-reverse fold one corner for the beak. Fold down the wings.

8 The finished Flapping Bird. Hold the bottom front and pull the tail in and out to make the wings flap!

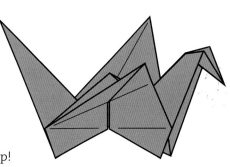

SKUNK

Designed by Michael G. LaFosse

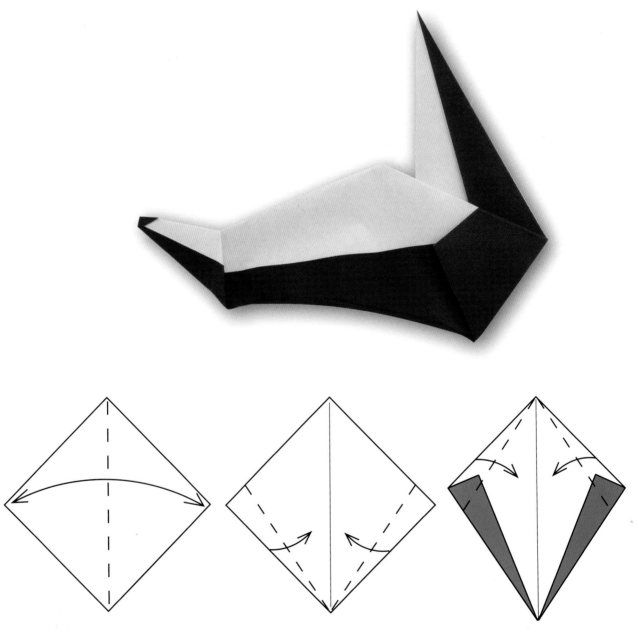

1 With the white side of the paper facing up, fold in half corner to corner. Unfold.

2 Fold in the bottom edges, but not all the way to the crease.

3 Fold in the top edges, the same amount as for the bottom.

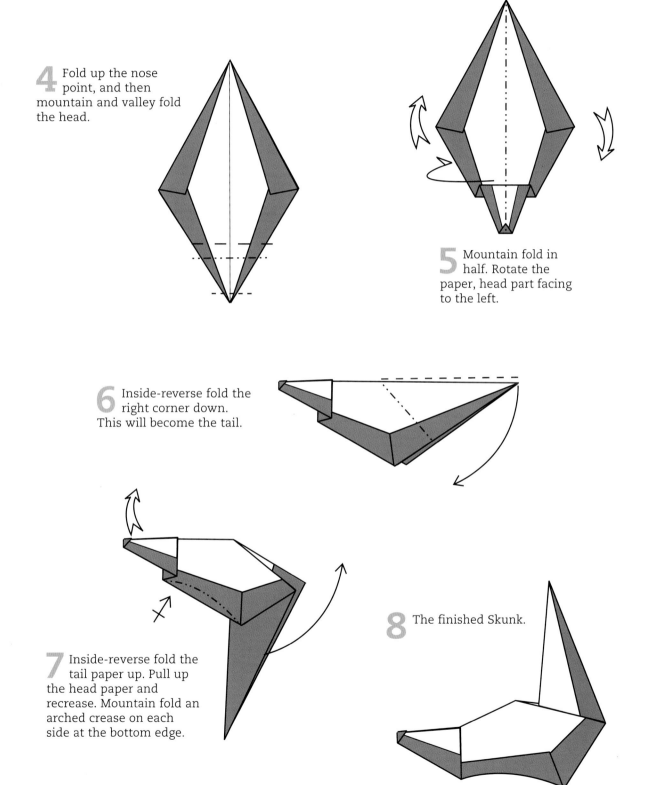

4 Fold up the nose point, and then mountain and valley fold the head.

5 Mountain fold in half. Rotate the paper, head part facing to the left.

6 Inside-reverse fold the right corner down. This will become the tail.

7 Inside-reverse fold the tail paper up. Pull up the head paper and recrease. Mountain fold an arched crease on each side at the bottom edge.

8 The finished Skunk.

PENGUIN

Designed by Michael G. LaFosse

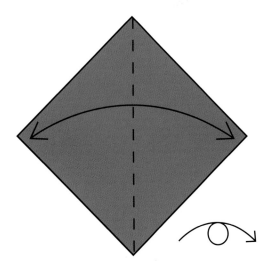

1 Begin with the black side up. Fold in half corner to corner. Unfold and turn over.

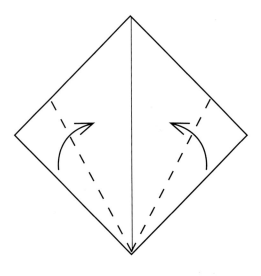

2 With the white side up, fold in the bottom edges, but not all the way to the crease.

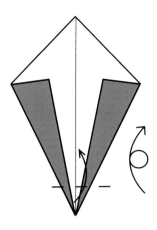

3 Fold up the bottom corner.
Turn over top to bottom.

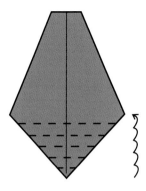

4 Fold up the bottom corner, over
and over, to make the bottom
edge flat and sturdy.

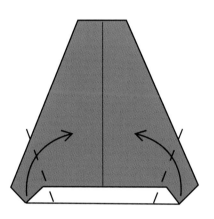

5 Fold the bottom corners in.

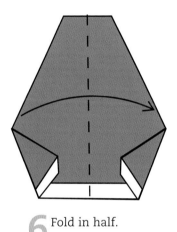

6 Fold in half.

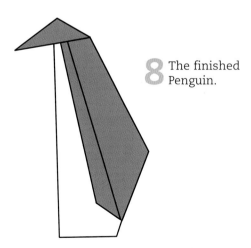

7 Pull up the beak.
Fold out the wings.

8 The finished
Penguin.

WHALE

Designed by Michael G. LaFosse

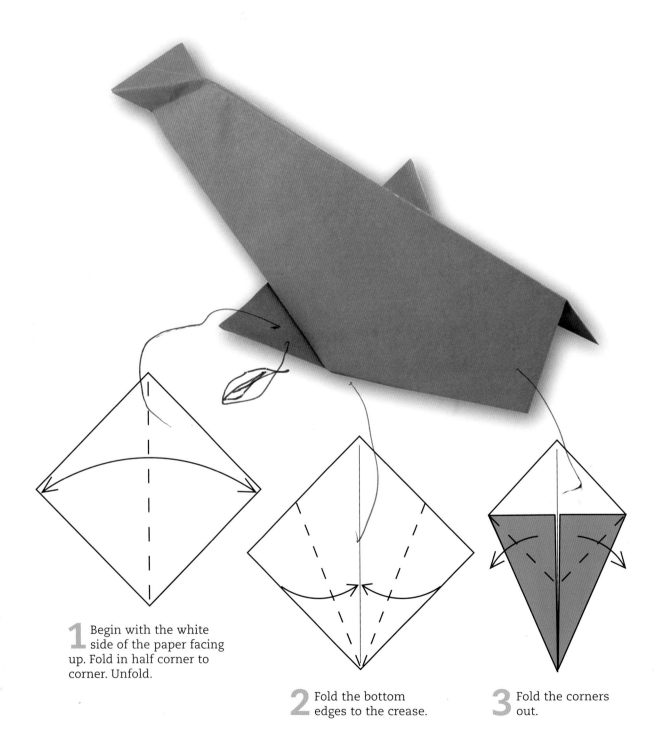

1 Begin with the white side of the paper facing up. Fold in half corner to corner. Unfold.

2 Fold the bottom edges to the crease.

3 Fold the corners out.

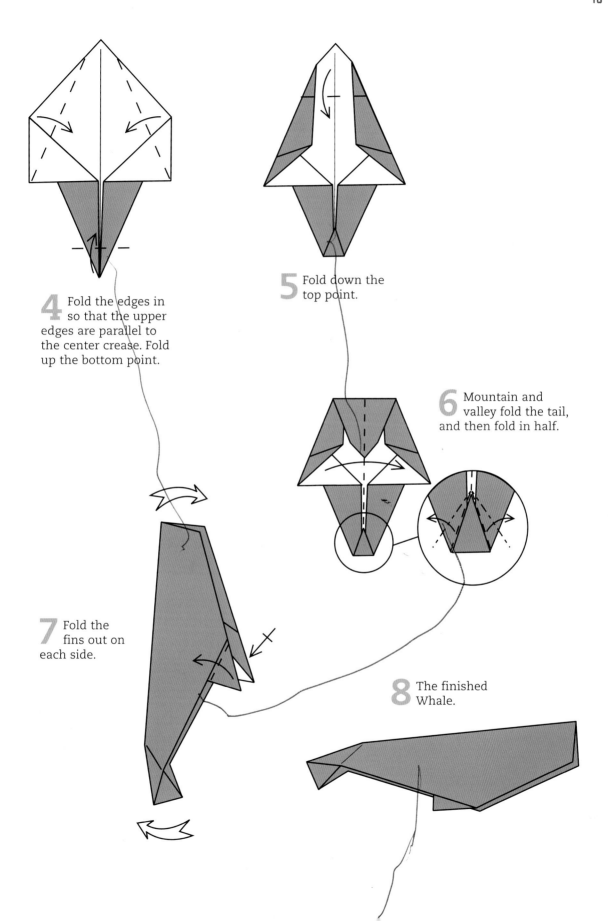

4 Fold the edges in so that the upper edges are parallel to the center crease. Fold up the bottom point.

5 Fold down the top point.

6 Mountain and valley fold the tail, and then fold in half.

7 Fold the fins out on each side.

8 The finished Whale.

BAT

Designed by Michael G. LaFosse

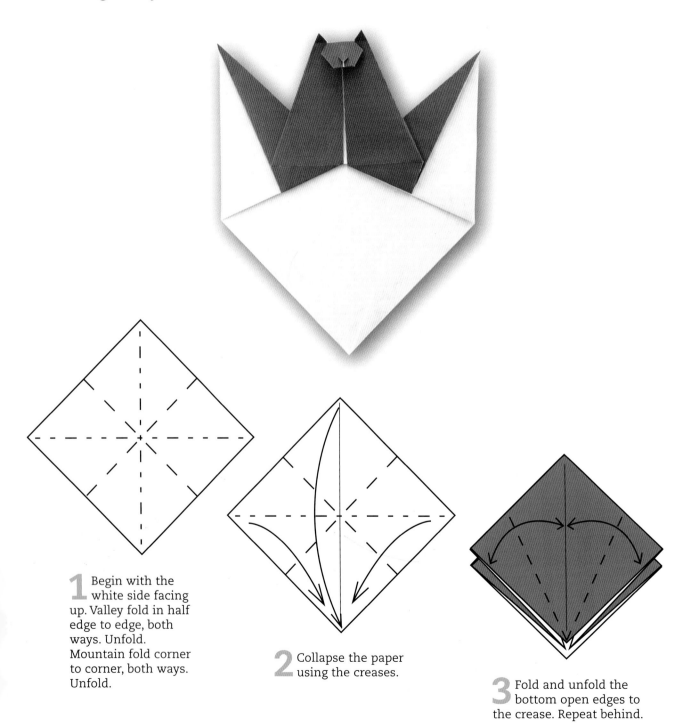

1 Begin with the white side facing up. Valley fold in half edge to edge, both ways. Unfold. Mountain fold corner to corner, both ways. Unfold.

2 Collapse the paper using the creases.

3 Fold and unfold the bottom open edges to the crease. Repeat behind.

4 Fold the bottom corner of the top layer all the way up while folding in the sides. Look at step 5 for the shape.

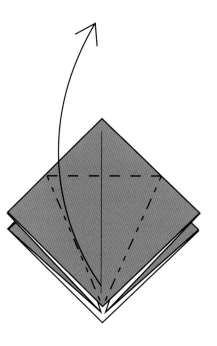

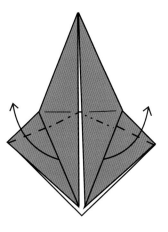

5 Inside-reverse fold the bottom corners up for wings.

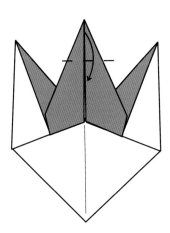

6 Fold down the top corner for the head.

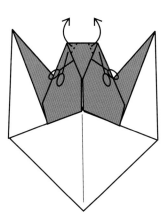

7 Cut the sides of the head for ears and stand them up.

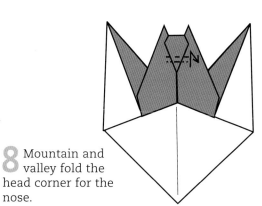

8 Mountain and valley fold the head corner for the nose.

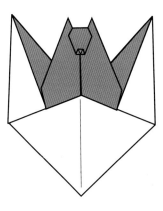

9 The finished Bat.

OWL

Designed by Michael G. LaFosse

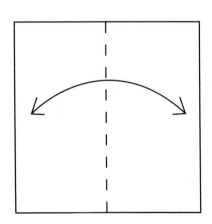

1 Begin with the white side facing up. Fold in half edge to edge. Unfold.

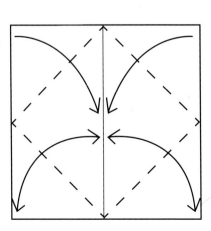

2 Fold all four corners to the center of the paper. Unfold the bottom two.

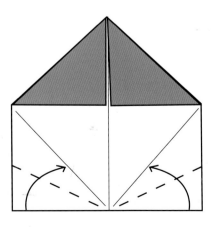

3 Fold the bottom edges up to the creases, left and right.

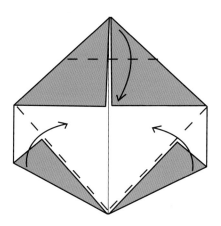

4 Fold down the top corner. Fold up the bottom edges.

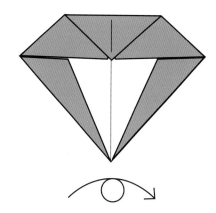

5 Your paper should look like this. Turn over, left to right.

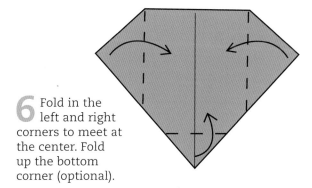

6 Fold in the left and right corners to meet at the center. Fold up the bottom corner (optional).

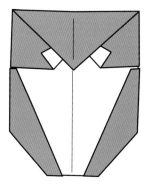

7 Turn over, left to right.

8 Fold over the two corners of paper that can be found under the beak—these will be the owl's eyes.

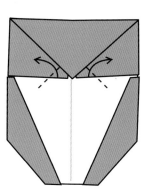

9 The finished Owl.

JAGUAR

Designed by Michael G. LaFosse

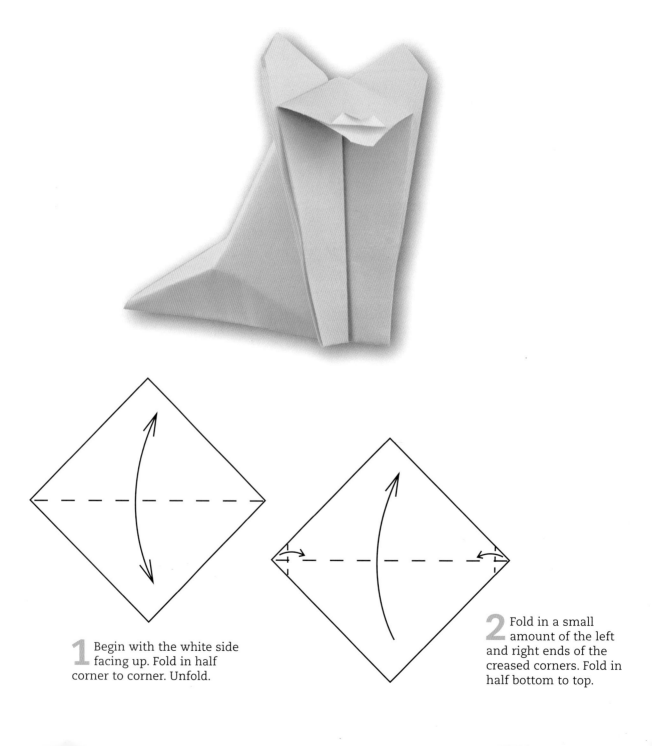

1 Begin with the white side facing up. Fold in half corner to corner. Unfold.

2 Fold in a small amount of the left and right ends of the creased corners. Fold in half bottom to top.

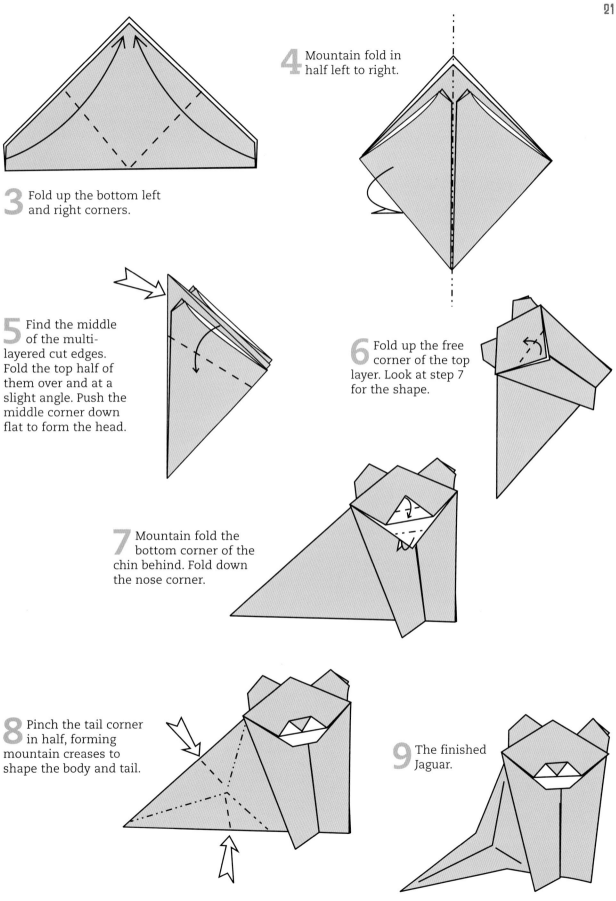

4 Mountain fold in half left to right.

3 Fold up the bottom left and right corners.

5 Find the middle of the multi-layered cut edges. Fold the top half of them over and at a slight angle. Push the middle corner down flat to form the head.

6 Fold up the free corner of the top layer. Look at step 7 for the shape.

7 Mountain fold the bottom corner of the chin behind. Fold down the nose corner.

8 Pinch the tail corner in half, forming mountain creases to shape the body and tail.

9 The finished Jaguar.

swan

Designed by Elsa Chen & Michael G. LaFosse

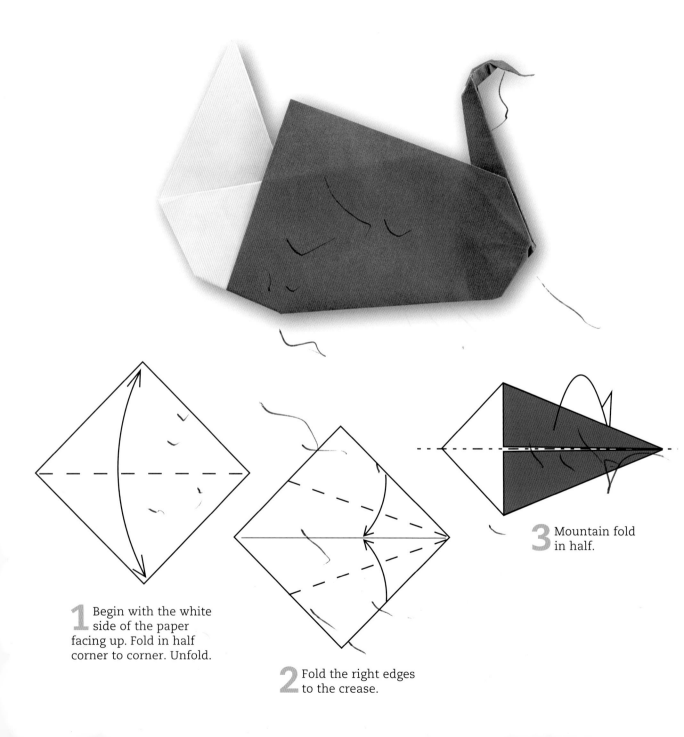

1 Begin with the white side of the paper facing up. Fold in half corner to corner. Unfold.

2 Fold the right edges to the crease.

3 Mountain fold in half.

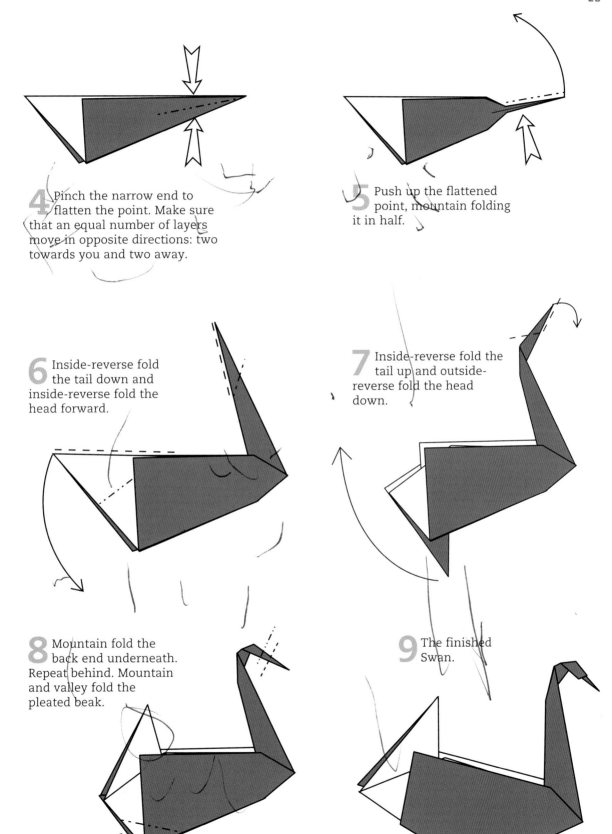

4 Pinch the narrow end to flatten the point. Make sure that an equal number of layers move in opposite directions: two towards you and two away.

5 Push up the flattened point, mountain folding it in half.

6 Inside-reverse fold the tail down and inside-reverse fold the head forward.

7 Inside-reverse fold the tail up and outside-reverse fold the head down.

8 Mountain fold the back end underneath. Repeat behind. Mountain and valley fold the pleated beak.

9 The finished Swan.

CRANE

Traditional Japanese design

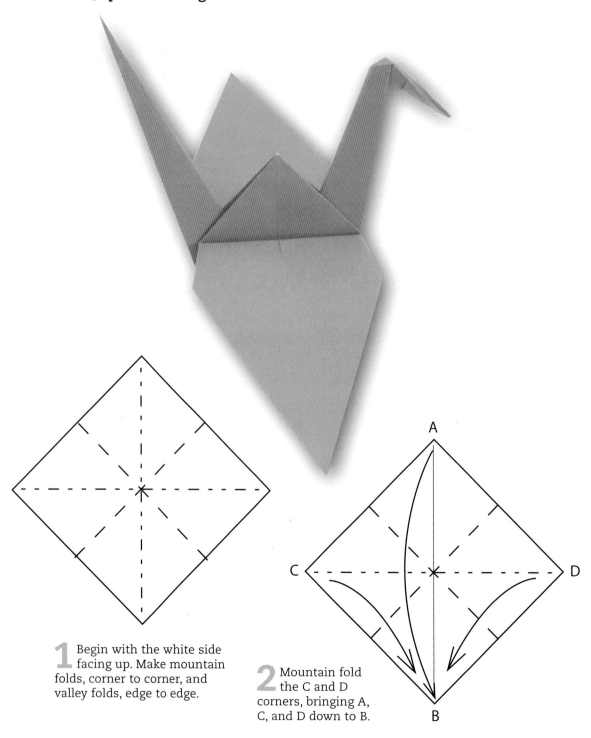

1 Begin with the white side facing up. Make mountain folds, corner to corner, and valley folds, edge to edge.

2 Mountain fold the C and D corners, bringing A, C, and D down to B.

3 Your paper should look like this. Fold and unfold the bottom open edges to the crease. Repeat behind.

4 Push in the corners, following the creases from step 3. Repeat behind.

5 Fold up the front flap. Repeat behind.

6 Fold in the bottom edges, two in the front and two in the back.

7 Inside-reverse fold the bottom corners.

8 Inside-reverse fold one corner for the beak. Fold down the wings.

9 The finished Crane.

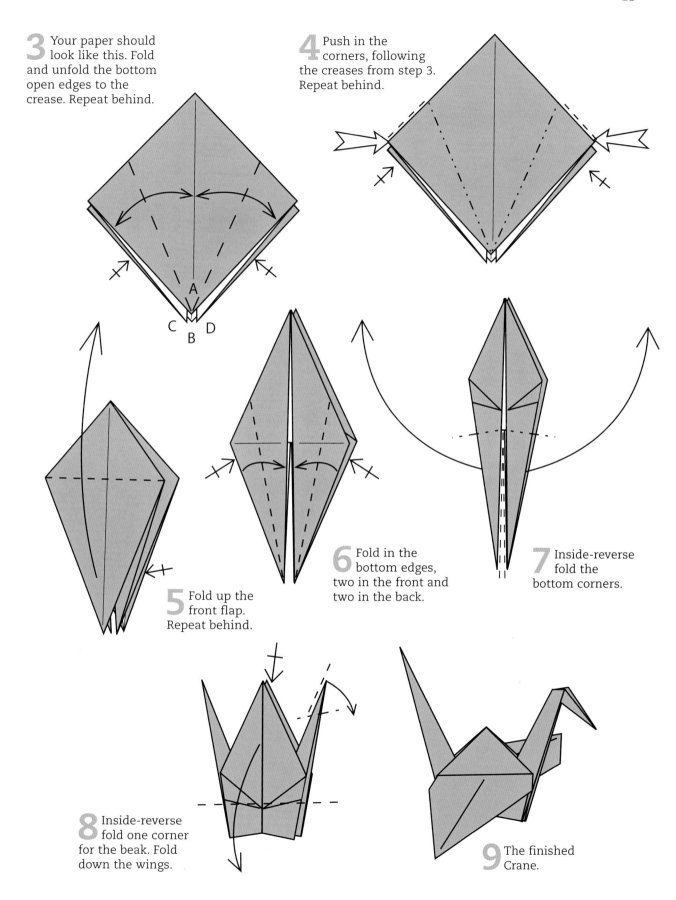

HORSESHOE CRAB

Designed by Michael G. LaFosse

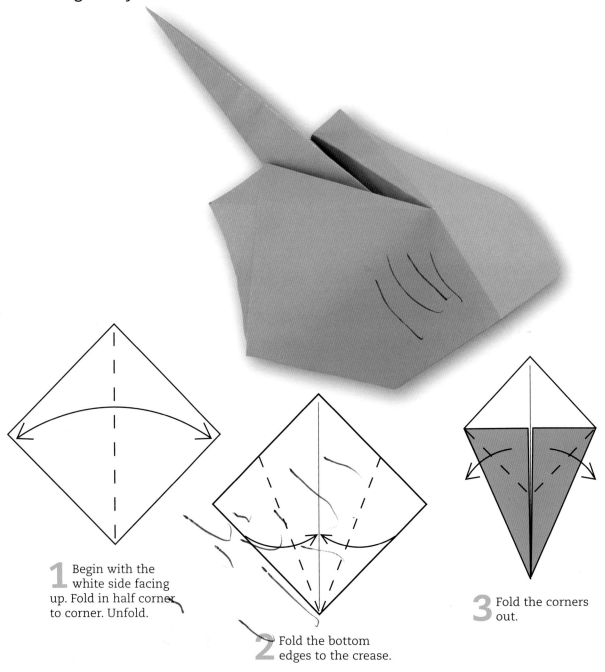

1 Begin with the white side facing up. Fold in half corner to corner. Unfold.

2 Fold the bottom edges to the crease.

3 Fold the corners out.

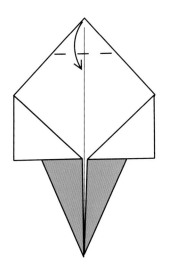

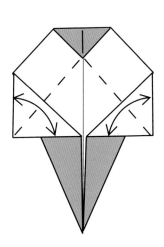

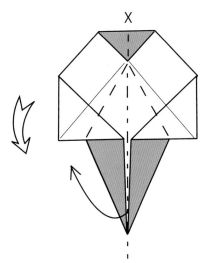

4 Fold the top corner down.

5 Valley fold the two square corners in half, making the creases meet at the center where the top point touches the crease. Unfold.

6 Inside-reverse fold the tail while folding the front in half.

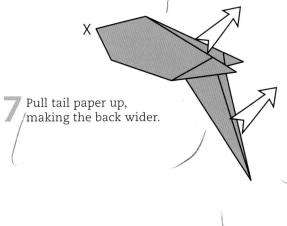

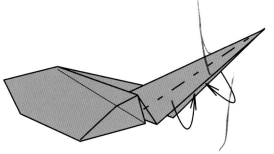

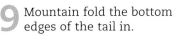

7 Pull tail paper up, making the back wider.

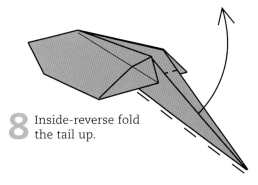

8 Inside-reverse fold the tail up.

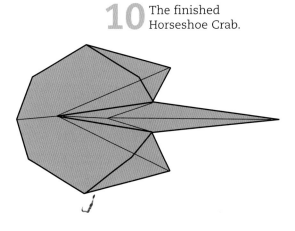

9 Mountain fold the bottom edges of the tail in.

10 The finished Horseshoe Crab.

BABY BIRD

Traditional Spanish design

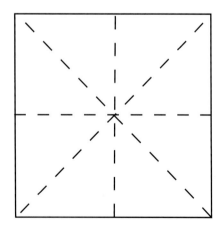

1 Begin with the white side facing up. Valley fold in half corner to corner and edge to edge.

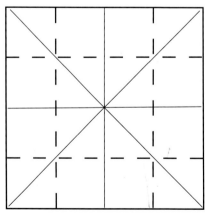

2 Fold and unfold each edge to the center. Turn over.

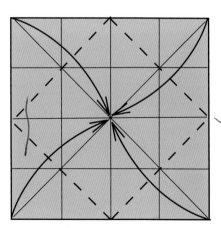

3 Fold all four corners to the center.

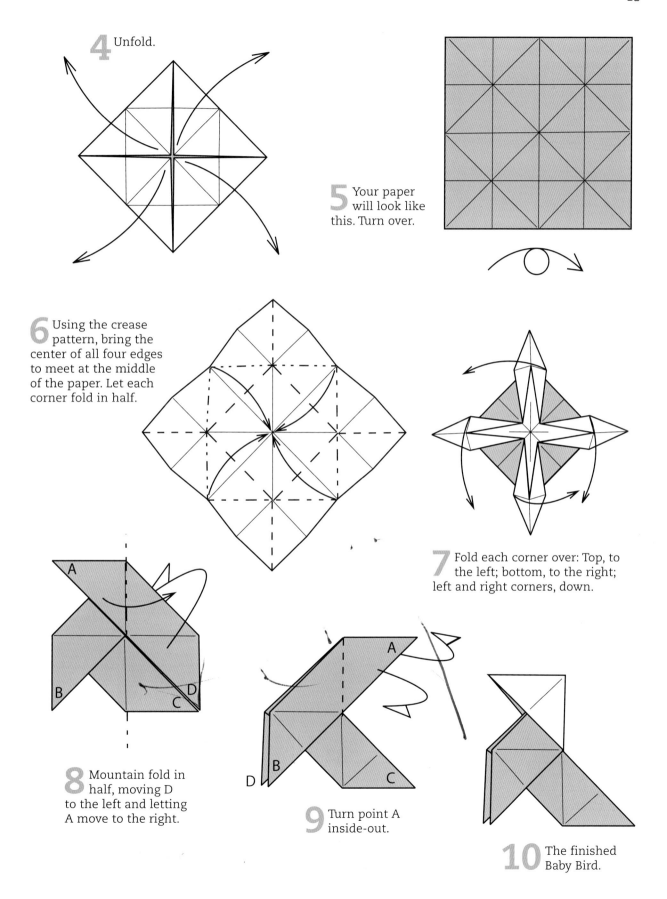

4 Unfold.

5 Your paper will look like this. Turn over.

6 Using the crease pattern, bring the center of all four edges to meet at the middle of the paper. Let each corner fold in half.

7 Fold each corner over: Top, to the left; bottom, to the right; left and right corners, down.

8 Mountain fold in half, moving D to the left and letting A move to the right.

9 Turn point A inside-out.

10 The finished Baby Bird.

TURTLE

Designed by Michael G. LaFosse

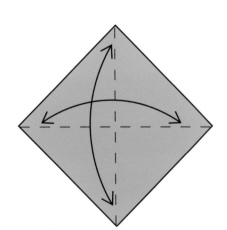

1 Begin color side up. Valley fold in half corner to corner, both ways. Unfold.

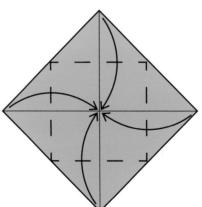

2 Fold all four corners to the center.

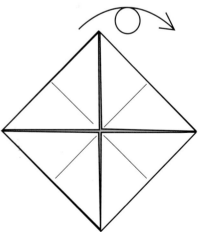

3 Your paper will look like this. Turn over.

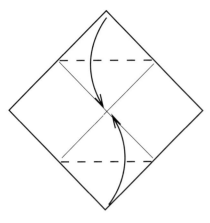

4 Fold the top and bottom corners in to the center.

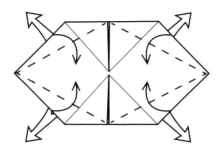

5 Fold in the left and right edges, allowing the corners of paper to come out from underneath.

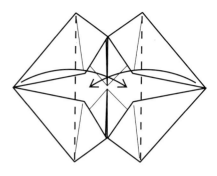

6 Fold over the right corner and then the left.

7 Fold the raw edges of the top triangular flap to match the folded edges, top and bottom, while folding the square corner to the left. Finish the shape by folding the free edges of the square corner to meet at the middle, narrowing the point. Repeat with the other flap to the right.

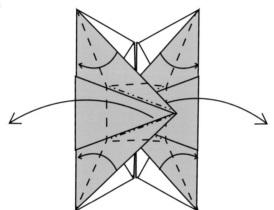

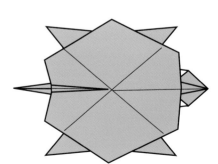

8 Fold out the top layers of the right point. Fold all four white corners in to the center.

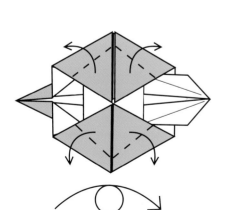

9 Fold the center corners out to create legs. Turn over.

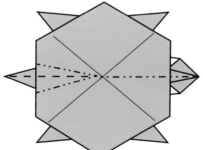

10 Mountain fold in half. Inside-reverse fold the tail.

11 The finished Turtle.

CHAMELEON

Designed by Michael G. LaFosse

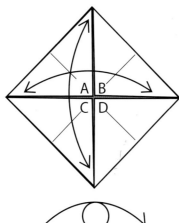

1 Fold steps 1 and 2 of the Turtle (see page 30). Fold in half corner to corner, both ways. Unfold. Turn over.

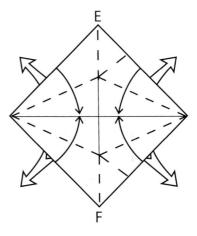

2 Fold in all four sides of the square to the center while folding corners E and F in half and then to the right. Allow the corners underneath to come out from behind.

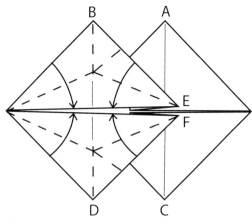

3 Fold in all four sides of the left square to the center while folding corners B and D in half and to the right.

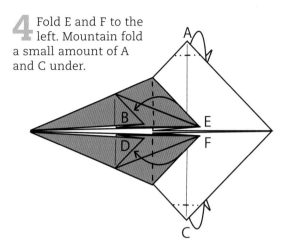

4 Fold E and F to the left. Mountain fold a small amount of A and C under.

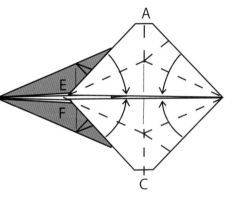

5 Fold in all four sides of the right square to the center while folding A and C in half and to the right.

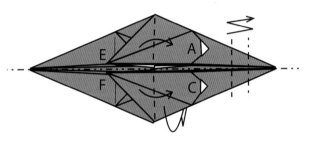

6 Fold E and F to the right. Mountain and valley fold the right corner to make the mouth. Mountain fold in half the long way.

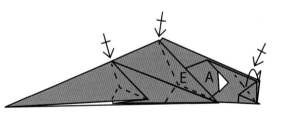

7 Make the legs by folding the corners in half and then down. Mountain fold the front corners of the head inside.

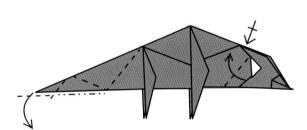

8 Fold up the eyes. Curl the tail with a series of outside- and inside-reverse folds.

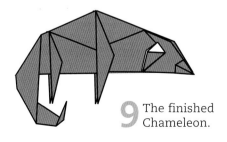

9 The finished Chameleon.

mouse

Designed by Michael G. LaFosse

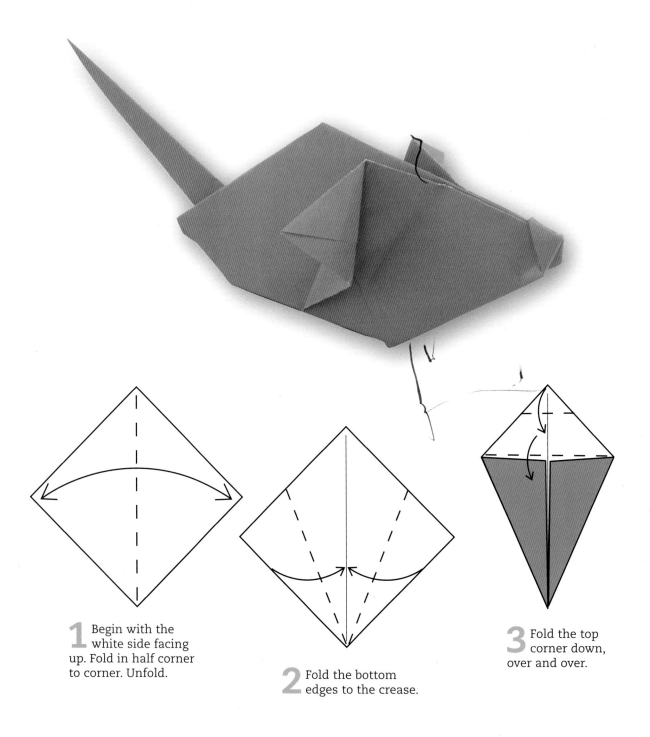

1 Begin with the white side facing up. Fold in half corner to corner. Unfold.

2 Fold the bottom edges to the crease.

3 Fold the top corner down, over and over.

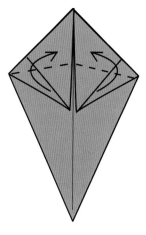

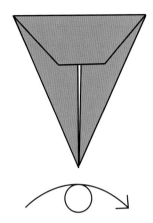

4 Your paper will look like this. Turn it over.

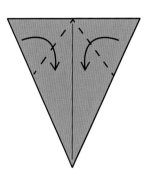

5 Fold down the top corners, making them meet at the crease.

6 Fold up the two corners for ears.

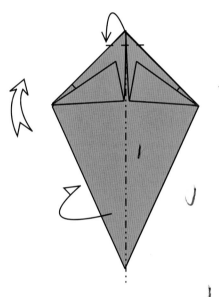

7 Fold the top corner down for the nose. Mountain fold the paper in half and rotate, nose to the right.

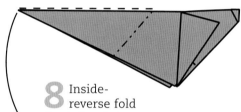

8 Inside-reverse fold the left point down for the tail.

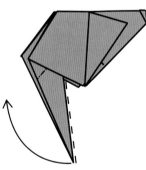

9 Inside-reverse fold the tail out to the left.

10 Mountain fold the bottom edges of the tail inside. Fold the bottom corners in. Fold and unfold the ears.

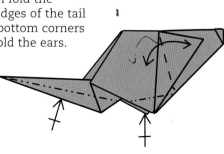

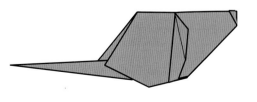

11 The finished Mouse.

CARP

Designed by Michael G. LaFosse

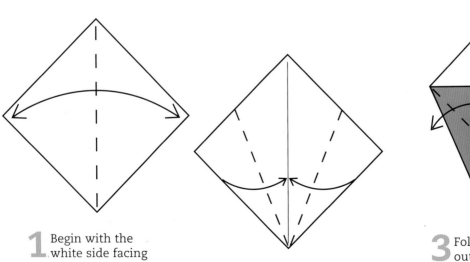

1 Begin with the white side facing up. Fold in half corner to corner. Unfold.

2 Fold the bottom edges to the crease.

3 Fold the corners out.

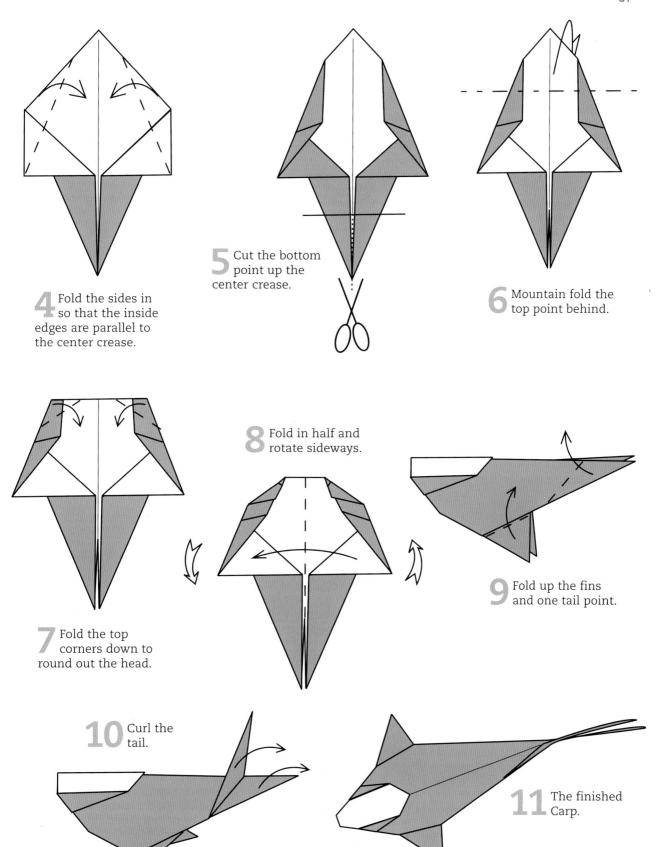

4 Fold the sides in so that the inside edges are parallel to the center crease.

5 Cut the bottom point up the center crease.

6 Mountain fold the top point behind.

7 Fold the top corners down to round out the head.

8 Fold in half and rotate sideways.

9 Fold up the fins and one tail point.

10 Curl the tail.

11 The finished Carp.

seal

Designed by Michael G. LaFosse

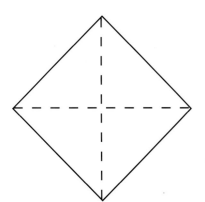

1 Begin with the white side facing up. Fold in half corner to corner, both ways. Unfold.

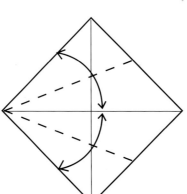

2 Fold the two left edges to meet at the crease. Unfold.

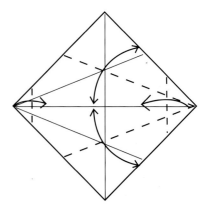

3 Fold the two right edges to meet at the crease. Unfold. Fold in the left corner a little bit. Fold the right corner in halfway to the middle of the paper.

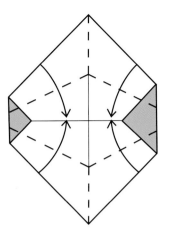

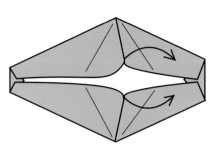

5 Fold the short corners to the right.

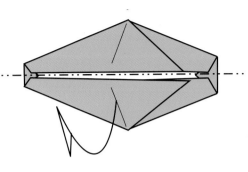

6 Your paper should look like this. Mountain fold in half behind, bottom corner to top.

4 Fold all four edges to meet at the horizontal crease. At the point where these folds meet, crease to the top and bottom corners. The model will not lie flat.

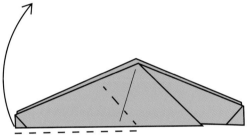

7 Inside-reverse fold the left end to form the neck.

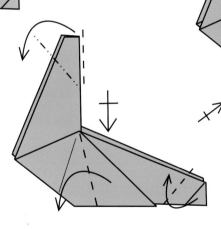

8 Inside-reverse fold the head. Fold the front flippers down toward the front end. Valley fold the right end up so that the bottom corner meets the slanted edge.

9 Fold up the ends of the front flippers to allow the model to stand. Squash fold the paper at the tail end.

10 Inside-reverse fold the back end to make it look forked, and then bend it back to the center.

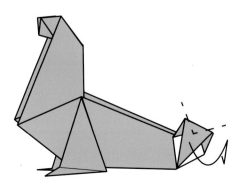

11 The finished Seal.

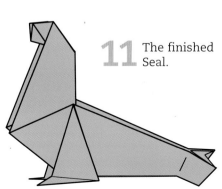

CARDINAL

Designed by Michael G. LaFosse

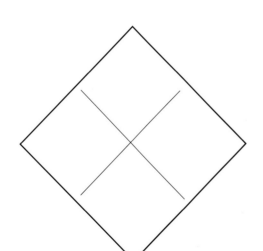

1 Begin with the white side facing up. Fold in half edge to edge, each way, to mark your paper with crossing creases.

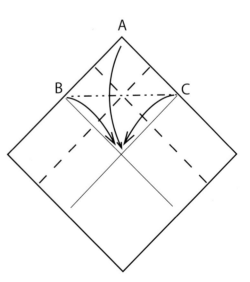

2 Fold the top edges to the crease lines and unfold. Fold the top corner to the center of the back and unfold. Use these mountain and valley creases to bring A, B, and C together.

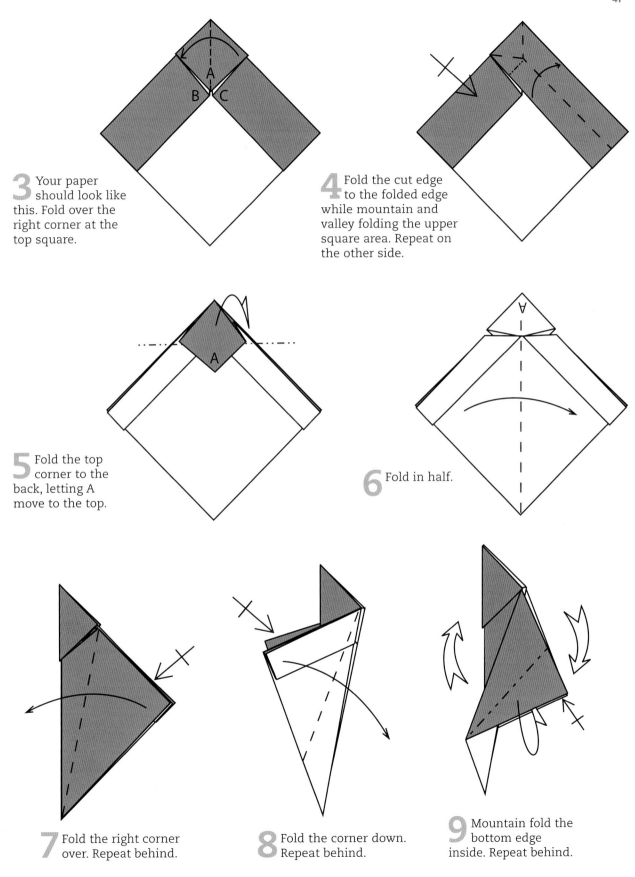

3 Your paper should look like this. Fold over the right corner at the top square.

4 Fold the cut edge to the folded edge while mountain and valley folding the upper square area. Repeat on the other side.

5 Fold the top corner to the back, letting A move to the top.

6 Fold in half.

7 Fold the right corner over. Repeat behind.

8 Fold the corner down. Repeat behind.

9 Mountain fold the bottom edge inside. Repeat behind.

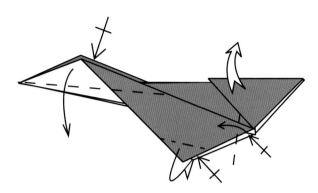

10 Fold the tail papers down on each side. Pull up on the crest of the head. Fold the bottom corners underneath.

11 Fold up the bottom corner of the head. Unfold and repeat behind.

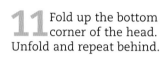

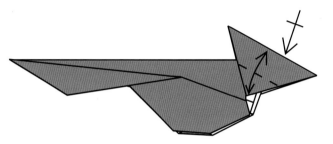

12 Fold the bottom right edge up to the crease, and then fold up again. Repeat behind.

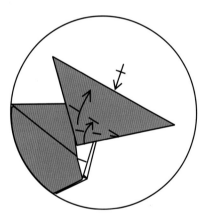

13 Mountain and valley fold the front corner to form the pleated beak.

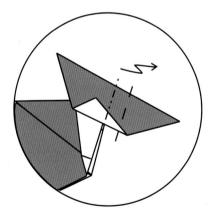

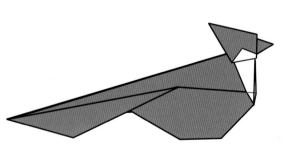

14 The finished Cardinal.

anteater

Designed by Michael G. LaFosse

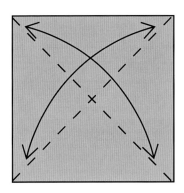

1 Begin color side up. Valley fold in half corner to corner, both ways. Unfold.

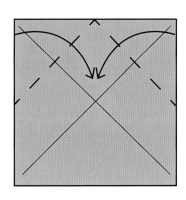

2 Fold the top two corners to the center.

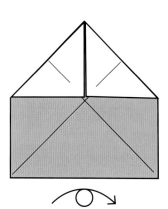

3 Turn over.

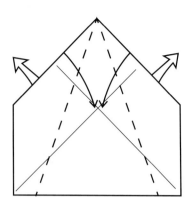

4 Fold in the top edges to meet in the middle. Allow the two corners to come out from underneath.

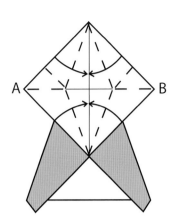

5 Fold in all four sides of the square to the center while folding corners A and B in half, and then up.

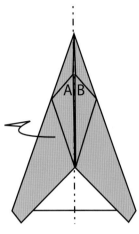

6 Mountain fold in half.

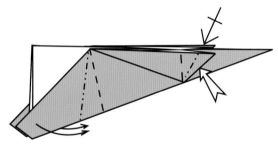

7 Squash fold the ears. Using the existing crease, mountain and valley fold the legs forward.

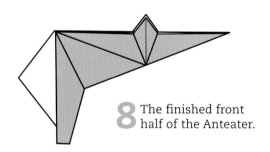

8 The finished front half of the Anteater.

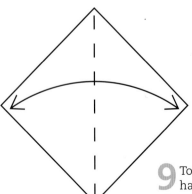

9 To make the back half, fold a new piece of paper (white side facing up) in half corner to corner. Unfold.

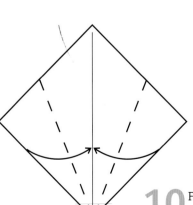

10 Fold in the bottom edges to meet at the center crease.

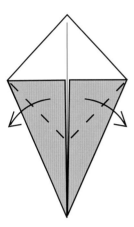

11 Fold out the two square corners.

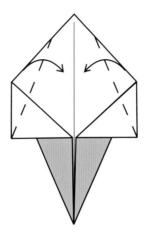

12 Fold the sides in so their vertical edges are parallel to the center crease.

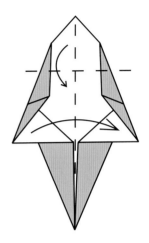

13 Fold down the top point. Fold the model in half.

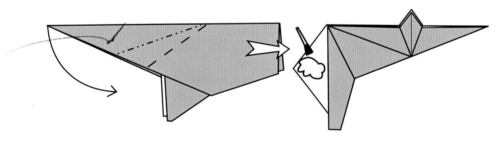

14 Paste the two ends together. Mountain and valley fold the tail.

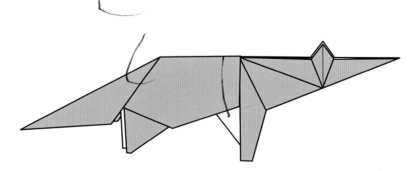

15 The finished Anteater.

HUMMINGBIRD

Designed by Michael G. LaFosse

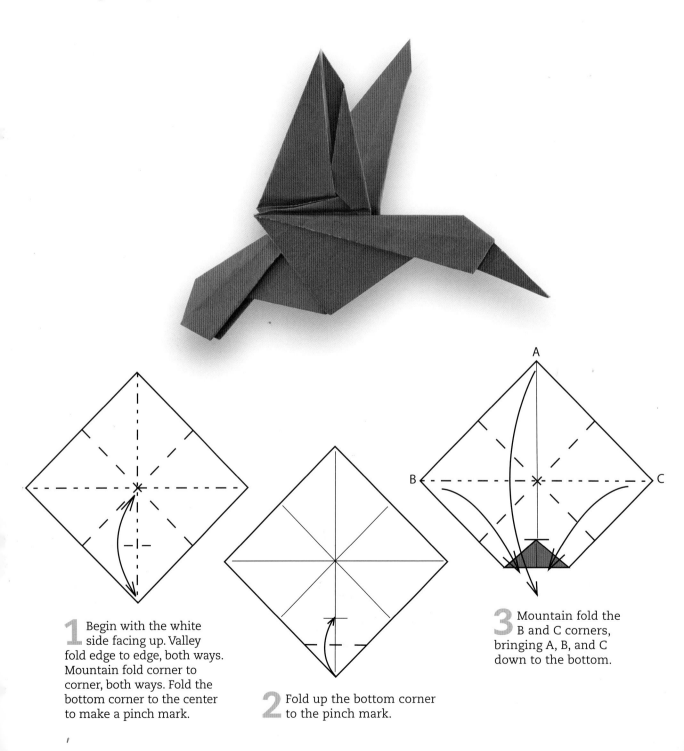

1 Begin with the white side facing up. Valley fold edge to edge, both ways. Mountain fold corner to corner, both ways. Fold the bottom corner to the center to make a pinch mark.

2 Fold up the bottom corner to the pinch mark.

3 Mountain fold the B and C corners, bringing A, B, and C down to the bottom.

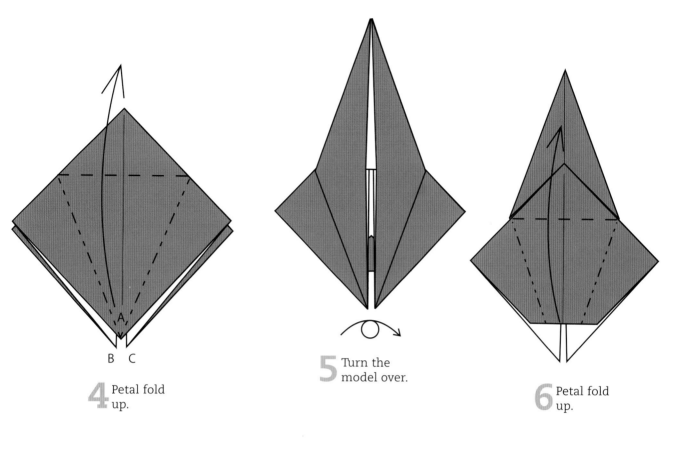

4 Petal fold up.

5 Turn the model over.

6 Petal fold up.

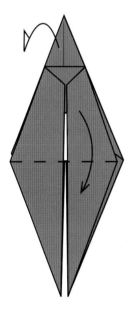

7 Bring top flaps back down, one on each side.

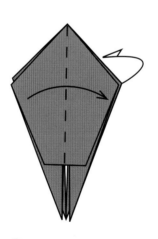

8 Reorient paper flaps: upper-left folds over to the right; lower-right folds over to the left.

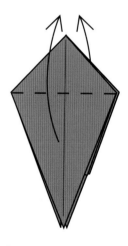

9 Bring front and back flaps up.

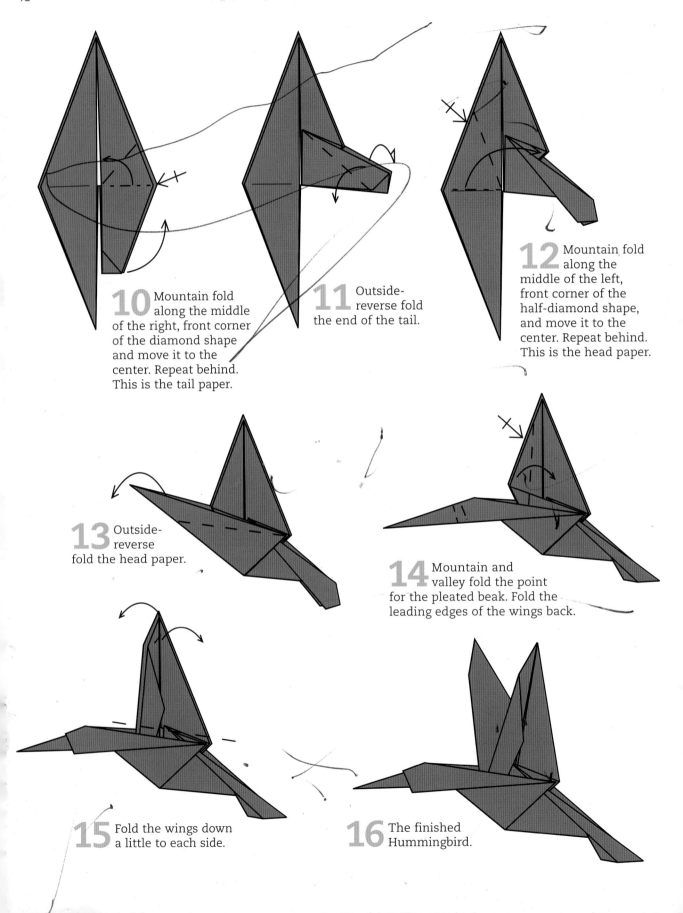

10 Mountain fold along the middle of the right, front corner of the diamond shape and move it to the center. Repeat behind. This is the tail paper.

11 Outside-reverse fold the end of the tail.

12 Mountain fold along the middle of the left, front corner of the half-diamond shape, and move it to the center. Repeat behind. This is the head paper.

13 Outside-reverse fold the head paper.

14 Mountain and valley fold the point for the pleated beak. Fold the leading edges of the wings back.

15 Fold the wings down a little to each side.

16 The finished Hummingbird.